I0621055

Embrace Curiosity, Self-Honesty, and Faith
as You Redefine Your Paths

THE
COACH
WITHIN

An Inspiring Guide that
Explores the Transformative
Power of Coaching

LEONA P. JACKSON

Author of The Spirit of Becoming

KP PUBLISHING COMPANY

ISBN: 978-1-960001-83-2 (Paperback)
ISBN: 978-1-960001-84-9 (eBook)

Library of Congress Control Number: Pending

Editor: Laurel J. Davis
Cover Design: Juan Roberts, Creative Lunacy
Literary Director: Sandra Slayton James

Published by:

KP Publishing Company
Publisher of Fiction, Nonfiction & Children's Books
Las Vegas, NV 89117
www.kp-pub.com

Printed in the United States of America

"AS"

By Stevie Wonder (1977)

This song is my tribute to the power of self-love.
"Self-love is a game-changer across the many strands of life."

—Leona P. Jackson

FOREWORD

Relentless defines Leona P. Jackson. Ms. Jackson faced a desire to lead by example and refused to accept defeat, searching for an internal or external instructor. Her literacy management skills provide powerful insights into her writing journey. She was the student, the instructor, the author, the client, and the coach—while her imagination introduced project after project to aid herself through the survival of many valleys of defeat and—mountains to climb to reach success.

As she faced many unsuccessful trials, she also faced successful rewards concerning her ongoing self-management, relationship management, and leadership management competencies. Her initial journey was undoubtedly filled with many complexities, uneasiness, and treacherous fears, but her emotional, social, and spiritual awareness rose to a higher level of competence.

Thank you, Ms. Jackson, for your endearing contributions toward leadership development and sharing culture values and vibes no matter what. I wish you well as you continue to strive, thrive, and continue to claim and reclaim your seat at the corporate tables of further development.

Secret Charles-Ford, Ed.D.

THE DIMENSIONS OF COACHING

COACHING PARTNERSHIP

One-to-one coaching is a distinctive partnership between people through shared humanity—coach and client—who work together as equals on a defined set of coachable goals. It is a confidential and in-depth dialogue to deepen a client's self–awareness and clarity.

COACHING GROUP INTERACTIONS

Group coaching and coaching by on-sight transformation is a distinctive partnership between a shared human experience—coach and individual seekers—who work together as equals on defined various coachable goals. It is a confidential and in-depth dialogue to deepen the coaching experience for the team's and groups' self–awareness and clarity.

THE COACH WITHIN (SELF-COACHING)

For me, self-coaching or (The Coach Within) is, as Albert Einstein allegedly defines insanity, doing the same things repeatedly and expecting different outcomes. *We understand this concept infinitely.* We also know that it is not easy to abandon old deep-rooted patterns. Self-coaching requires one to have acquired a skeptical, curious, and sufficient degree of transparency, hope, and faith to explore an external coaching tool to think more resounding, think differently, think more genuinely, and grasp the willingness to abide by the acceptance of their phenomenal newfound truths to further build upon.

"A leader knows the way, goes the way, and shows the way."

−John C. Maxwell

PREFACE

SURRENDERING TO SOBRIETY

I surrendered to sobriety—to be exact, on May 3, 1977, and each day since. Before that date, 47 years ago, I did not know the term sobriety, let alone all that it offers: abstinence, order, and the underlying rudiments of self-honesty. What I did know was that I felt Hopeless.

It seemed like from age 17 to 30, struggling not to drink had become an obsession. I also possessed a lingering desire to know what having hope felt like. And I wondered how hope was adopted or formed within. No one I asked could articulate what "hope" meant; this made me sadder than sad as Smoky Robinson and The Miracles sing in the song—"The Tears of a Clown." From a very early age, I always wanted someone to tell me what having "hope and faith meant.

Most seniors were quick to reiterate the partial scripture,

"Faith without works is dead."

James 2:26 (KJV)

And that one only needed faith of the size of a mustard seed to move mountains. These statements made me feel even more distressed. Being unaware of the power of hope and faith became a nightmare.

On the other hand, I was a courageous young person once upon a time, but by age twelve, I had become a non-bravery soul, and it was impossible to wrap my mind around self-honesty. At twenty-five, I checked myself into a Wellness establishment by chance. On one of the seven days I was there, one of the clinicians addressed a group of us about bravery and non-bravery strategies. I had wanted to talk about my misplaced courage with someone at least thirteen years before turning twenty-five. I sensed evidence of my lost courage slowly returning anonymously by the end of 1977.

At this point of surrender, I believed my misplaced courage was re-entering my life and it was. My integrity was slow to identify itself. However, I knew I had touched bases with integrity in the first 30, 60, or 90 days of sobriety. It was years later before I learned a working definition of "integrity," aligning your conduct with what you know to be excellence and displaying principled dedication to core values and honorable beliefs.

I struggled and fought the willingness to want to change; it seemed taboo to surrender to change for many years. I believe true humility is a gift from a power greater than us. Another anonymous friend gave me a working definition of humility — a rising in spirit.

I learned that Love is a physiological motivation and a healing balm. Self-discipline is having control over one's actions and thoughts. Perseverance, I discovered, is—not giving up faster than lightning in difficult decision-making moments.

I am realizing self-awareness is having the wisdom to know who you are, whose you are, and who you are not.

Service is the action of helping or doing work for someone.

When you're on the path to overcoming obsessions, understanding the true meaning of sobriety is crucial. Sobriety extends beyond the absence of mood-altering substances in your system; it's a multidimensional journey toward overall wellness.

In its essence, sobriety means living a life not controlled by substances but instead guided by a clear and present commitment to health, wellness, relationships, self-awareness, and personal development. It means detaching from the past drama and living in a self-disciplined, safe space.

I believe sobriety means living by principal practices. I ultimately received my answers from much divine and natural research and studying, as well as from—The Coach Within.

—The Coach Within

CONTENTS
THE COACH WITHIN
12 PRINCIPLES

Chapter 1

SURRENDERING TO SELF-HONESTY

Self-honesty is the practice of always speaking and
acting in accordance with what you believe to be true,
even if it's unpleasant or inconvenient. It involves being
honest with yourself about your thoughts, feelings, and actions,
and recognizing your limitations and facing your fears.

—Merriam/Webster

One of my first authentic moments of surrendering to transparency came when I glanced at the condition of my hands. It was 1964 and had just been dismissed from the family's hauling business. I was sixteen. Staring at my working man's hands, I was in shock. I lost my breath for a second or so; I wanted to scream, run, or hide my hands from me. Finally, I took a deep breath and evaluated the induced traumatizing sight of my hands. The setup was unfortunate; *I had to live [with]*

1

myself, so I wanted to take steps to become fit for myself to know! That day had finally arrived!

My hands were far from beautiful, and I had to acknowledge this truth and begin caring for my entire self, not just my hands. I had to accept my external repairs before starting my inner reconstruction. The following years became continuous nightmares of rejecting and accepting this reality and other unacceptable, dislikeable aspects of myself. This surrendering moment took years to fully accept as I worked on healing the many damages, one area of my body at a time. There was an old spiritual song back in the day. One of the lyrics was, "I looked at my hands, and they looked new, I looked at my feet, and they did too, and ever since that wonderful day, my soul has been satisfied." At that time, I wondered what "my soul has been satisfied" meant.

Dealing with what is known, I recognized early on that I needed guidance. From as early as six years old, I sought a source of wisdom to help me avoid life's pitfalls. Yet, life remained an ongoing challenge. Striving to get it right was difficult, and at seventy-eight, I still found myself swinging between acceptance and frustration.

Self-honesty is about becoming the best version of yourself, even amid chaos and uncertainty. It's the ability to look at the reality of your life, acknowledge your flaws and fears, and commit to growing through it all. When life is most unpredictable, it's honesty with yourself that provides the foundation for transformation. Chaos doesn't define you—your willingness to face it does. When you're honest with yourself, you create room for clarity, courage, and the strength to rise above even the most turbulent circumstances.

In 1977, I finally admitted that I had wasted years trying to fix my life. My choices had led me down a path of self-destruction, filled with failed attempts and repeated mistakes. No one had told me that true success and peace required more than effort—it demanded a spirit transformation. When I finally surrendered to God, something greater than myself, I found the clarity and direction I'd been missing.

Surrendering to self-honesty became my saving grace and my ride and live friend. I embraced my fears and began to trust in faith, gradually finding a balance between fear and hope. Over time, I realized that holding on to fear closed me off while letting go of it allowed faith to grow. As I let go of the past, I felt more liberated and open to living with purpose and passion.

Coaching, at its core, is about life. It's about helping people recognize their potential and make decisions aligned with their values and goals.

As a coach, I learned to celebrate small achievements, often leading to more significant milestones. Effective decision-making is not easy, but it is a skill that we can develop with practice. Blame, on the other hand, keeps us trapped in defensiveness. Actual change only happens when we let go of the need to blame and embrace our responsibility.

Today, insults, wrong choices, offenses, nonsense, folly, duplicity, and trickery does not hold my mind hostage to past events as they once did. Hope has led me out of the wilderness of obsessively rehearsing what's wrong and redirected me toward a more meaningful light, which instills within me what is right day by day. Thank you, God.

GRATITUDE AS A COACH EMBRACING THE GIFT OF HELPING OTHERS TRANSFORM THEIR LIVES

Gratitude is a powerful force that can enrich every aspect of life, and as a coach, it holds an extraordinary place. The journey of coaching guides others to recognize the privilege of playing such a significant role in someone's transformation. As a coach, you can witness people at their most vulnerable, courageous, and authentic selves. This profound responsibility serves as growth as you experience alongside them.

The practice of gratitude in coaching is essential because it shapes our perspectives and increases our energy. When we approach our work from a place of gratitude, we create a ripple effect that positively influences ourselves and our clients. Gratitude fosters patience, empathy, and a genuine connection, making the coaching relationship more profound and impactful. It allows us to stay grounded, even in challenging moments and reminds us of the larger purpose of our work. Each session becomes an opportunity to guide our clients and reflect on the immense value of helping navigate the change and growth journey.

As we close this chapter, it feels only fitting to reflect on all twelve principles, embracing their positivity now that we've surrendered the stubborn will to cling to mental injuries long after the offenses have passed. We've discovered that self-honesty opens the door to more profound hope, strengthening our capacity for extraordinary acts of faith. Courage becomes a daily practice, integrity transforms our will, intentions, and willingness sparks unexpected shifts in our attitudes.

Resting in the spirit of love brings comfort and joy, while forgiveness is a deeply personal and liberating reward. Self-discipline shapes a new and fulfilling way of life, and self-awareness sharpens greater understanding of our motives, intentions, and actions. Finally, through the practice of service, we learn the beauty of giving and receiving, expressing gratitude for the ultimate gift giver. These principles illuminate a path toward growth, healing, and inner peace.

ACTIONABLE PRACTICE QUESTIONS

1. Recall a recent moment when you struggled with self-honesty. What held you back, and what did you learn?

_____

_____

_____

_____

2. What parts of yourself are most challenging to accept, and how embracing them bring?

_____

_____

_____

_____

3. Identify one area in which you're avoiding the truth. What's one small step toward acknowledging it?

_____

_____

_____

_____

4. Do you feel comfortable about your life and why?

_____

_____

_____

_____

5. How does fear limit you, and what's one way to let go and invite more faith?

_____

_____

_____

_____

Chapter 2

SURRENDERING TO HOPE

Hope is an optimistic state of mind that is based on
an expectation of positive outcomes with respect to events
and circumstances in one's own life, or the world at large.

—Merrian /Webster

Looking back, I had always been my coach. At four or five years of age, I was walking out the back door of our first of five childhood homes when a thought came to me: *I was devoid of emotions.* Although unfamiliar with "emotions or feelings," I knew I felt bland and empty. My feelings were mixed up, like laughing when I should have been crying, running when I should have been standing still, and humming when I should have been thinking. Even today, my emotions get twisted. I later learned that this state was called numb. Yes, I was indeed sensationless, without any feelings except hot and cold.

We owned a swing set at the time. Even at that young age, I was trying to address my numbness. I intended to swing as high as possible to see what would happen. I moved my legs in and out repeatedly, going higher and higher until I came dangerously close—a fraction of an inch—to the top of the swing frame in mid-air.

Suddenly, I became aware that something unexpected would happen if I went any higher than the top of the swing set. On the next upward ride, the frame tilted backward, slightly shuddering forward, and I felt in danger for the first time. A simmering, violent shaking told me I was overswinging my bounds. I stopped moving my legs, and soon, it was safe to vacate the seat. Whoever had positioned the swing set in the yard had not cemented the legs for safety.

At seventeen years old, I began to drink for no apparent reason. After leaving home at sixteen, the next step seemed emotionally and physically challenging. Drinking seemed like a solution, an outline, a pattern, a path, a system, or a design by which one would arrive at adulthood with an already practiced and ultimately well-developed design for healthy living. Eye-catching ads in popular magazines of the sixties, seventies, and eighties like Jet, Ebony, and Essence, reinforced this idea. But this idea was entirely different from my case.

By thirty, I lacked self-discipline, hope, or emotional strength. There was an old saying back in the day: "Anyway, the wind blows, is cool with me!" That may be true on some higher level, but not for us, the defeated ones. I was moving closer and closer to three strikes—and you're out, out into total lostness like a ship on a raging sea of discontentment.

Through my journey, I have learned that there are intrinsic and extrinsic motivators. Intrinsic motivators drive internal desires to achieve, while extrinsic motivators drive external rewards and impact on long-term engagement. I have now learned to identify motivational techniques for determining what uniquely motivates one client (myself), including values exploration and motivational interviewing.

I feel like I cheated because I became my first known client! I was both the Coach and Client, and it remained that way for some seventy-eight years, up to the present. I have learned that interdependent mindset equals a high-performance mindset.

One of Daniel Goleman's seminal works, Emotional Intelligence, was published in 1995. It presents emotional intelligence as an acceptable, desirable, and necessary business tool. Emotional intelligence is the ability to relate to others from a paradigm of trust rather than fear, and it, therefore, sits firmly in the interdependent sector. More simply put, it's about having excellent personal and social skills.

Goleman and others have defined many competencies, including self-confidence, empathy, adaptability, and being a change catalyst. These can be grouped into four domains of emotional intelligence: self-awareness, self-management, social awareness, and relationship management.

In the journey toward emotional mastery, surrendering to hope is a powerful tool for transformation. As a life coach, guiding others to embrace the uncertainties of life requires an understanding that hope is not passive is a choice. By surrendering to hope, we allow ourselves to release control over the uncontrollable and trust the growth process. Managing emotions becomes a more fluid experience when we realize that hope enables us to weather storms with resilience rather than resisting them with fear. Through this lens, hope is an anchor, keeping us grounded in the belief that better days are possible, no matter the difficulties.

From a psychological perspective, managing emotions requires a balance between self-awareness and practical coping mechanisms. Surrendering to hope means embracing a mind shift, where negative emotional patterns are acknowledged but not allowed to dictate one's experience. By incorporating positive psychology techniques, individuals can foster a hopeful outlook that promotes well-being, self-discipline, and personal growth, ultimately leading to greater emotional freedom.

LIVING IN GRATITUDE:
HOW IT SHAPES YOU AS A COACH

Ultimately, living in gratitude as a coach transforms the coaching experience "if only we're brave enough to see it and brave enough to be it," Amanda Gorman says. Gratitude keeps us grounded, helps us navigate the emotional demands, and strengthens our connection to clients. It fosters resilience and compassion, allowing you to approach every situation with a mindset of abundance rather than scarcity. By cultivating gratitude, you enhance your coaching skills and model an essential practice for your clients.

In the end, hope is more than just a feeling; it's a way of living and working that shapes how you see the world and your role. As a coach, when you lead with gratitude, you create an environment filled with positivity, hope, and possibility—where you and your clients can thrive.

As we close this chapter, it feels only fitting to reflect on all twelve principles, embracing their positivity now that we've surrendered the stubborn will to cling to mental injuries long after the offenses have passed. We've discovered that self-honesty opens the door to more profound hope, strengthening our capacity for extraordinary acts of faith. Courage becomes a daily practice, integrity transforms our will, intentions, and willingness sparks unexpected shifts in our attitudes.

Resting in the spirit of love brings comfort and joy, while forgiveness is a deeply personal and liberating reward. Self-discipline shapes a new and fulfilling way of life, and self-awareness sharpens greater understanding of our motives, intentions, and actions. Finally, through the practice of service, we learn the beauty of giving and receiving, expressing gratitude for the ultimate gift giver. These principles illuminate a path toward growth, healing, and inner peace.

ACTIONABLE PRACTICE QUESTIONS

1. Recall a time when you felt numb or hopeless. What small steps helped you reconnect with your emotions?

_____

_____

_____

_____

2. How does hope influence your response to life's challenges? Describe one way to cultivate it actively.

_____

_____

_____

_____

3. What motivates you most—internal desires or external rewards? How can recognizing this improve your growth?

_____

_____

_____

_____

4. When have you allowed fear to overshadow hope? How might you choose to hope to change your perspective?

_____

_____

_____

_____

5. Identify one gratitude practice you can integrate daily. How could it shape your journey toward resilience?

_____

_____

_____

_____

Chapter 3

SURRENDERING TO FAITH

Faith is confidence or trust in a person, thing, or concept.

—Merriam/Webster

What would surrendering to faith look like? It would look like accepting the things we cannot change and changing the things we can. It would be like aligning our purpose to meet with the world's needs. In building my coaching practice I aim to empower and support my clients with the tools to unburden themselves, release unhealthy triggers, detach from negativity, and let go of what no longer serves them. At the same time, clients will develop their strategic decision-making processes, fostering more significant strength-based faith curiosity, compassion, clarity, confidence, calmness, creativity, courage, and connectiveness. Together, we will learn to align our core values with ongoing goals while striving to live principled lives.

I am a storyteller reflecting on my journey. Many of the stories I created by accident didn't align with what I wanted, nor was I ready for the outcomes they brought. Here's one of those accidental stories: in pursuit of a healthier lifestyle, I found myself in cosmetology school, learning a skill, I was hesitant about—something meant for me, others, and the world. Along the way to becoming a salon owner, I made several choices that ultimately impeded my undefined goal. Consequently, I reluctantly moved away from that intent with a bittersweet ending!

Effective coaching is built on advanced communication skills. These skills enable us to connect deeply, understand more fully, and guide us toward desired outcomes. Continuously honing these abilities enriches the relationships and interactions across all aspects of life. Coaching, in turn, enhances the client's capacity to identify challenges, set goals and act—sooner rather than later.

Creativity is about inventing, reinventing, growing, experimenting, taking risks (and sometimes not), remaking rules, breaking them, ignoring them, making mistakes, fixing those mistakes, occasionally having fun and sometimes getting frustrated.

As a coach, surrendering to faith means embracing the belief that each client has within them the potential for growth and transformation. It's about trusting the coaching process and the client's innate ability to find answers. When we surrender to faith, we let go of our need to control outcomes and instead focus on creating a safe, supportive environment where clients can explore, discover, and evolve at their own pace. This surrender allows us to be fully present with our clients, listening deeply and asking powerful questions that unlock new insights and possibilities.

Surrendering to faith also involves trusting our intuition and expertise as coaches. It means having confidence in our ability to guide clients through challenging moments, even when the path forward isn't clear. By modeling this trust and faith in the process, we inspire our clients to do the same. As they witness our unwavering belief in their potential, they cultivate that same faith in themselves. This mutual surrender to faith creates a powerful synergy in the coaching relationship, often leading to breakthroughs and transformations that surpass both the coach's and the client's initial expectations.

SAVING SPACE FOR SELF AS A COACH: THE ART OF PRESERVING YOUR ENERGY AND WELL-BEING

As a life coach, our calling is to hold space and ask powerful questions So, clients can become motivated to find their answers from within. Yes, this was news to me too. Their personal growth and transformation. However, this sacred work often requires an outpouring of emotional, mental, and spiritual energy, and if not carefully managed, it can deplete your inner reserves. In the quest to help others, it's easy to overlook your needs, neglecting the vital space required for self-reflection, rejuvenation, and growth. Saving space for self is not just about self-care; it's about recognizing that you, too, deserve the time and energy you pour into others. By preserving your well-being, you can show up more authentically, sustainably, and effectively as a coach.

As we close this chapter, it feels only fitting to reflect on all twelve principles, embracing their positivity now that we've surrendered the stubborn will to cling to mental injuries long after the offenses have passed. We've discovered that self-honesty opens the door to more profound hope, strengthening our capacity for extraordinary acts of faith. Courage becomes a daily practice, integrity transforms our will, intentions, and willingness sparks unexpected shifts in our attitudes.

Resting in the spirit of love brings comfort and joy, while forgiveness is a deeply personal and liberating reward. Self-discipline shapes a new and fulfilling way of life, and self-awareness sharpens greater understanding of our motives, intentions, and actions. Finally, through the practice of service, we learn the beauty of giving and receiving, expressing gratitude for the ultimate gift giver. These principles illuminate a path toward growth, healing, and inner peace.

ACTIONABLE PRACTICE QUESTIONS

1. Reflect on a recent situation where you trusted the process rather than controlling the outcome. What did you learn?

_____

_____

_____

_____

2. How can you align your core values with your goals better this week?

_____

_____

_____

_____

3. Identify an area where you're holding back out of fear. How might surrendering to faith open up new possibilities?

_____

_____

_____

_____

4. How do you preserve your energy as a coach? List one action you can take to care for yourself today.

_____

_____

_____

_____

5. Recall a time when you helped someone else grow. How did your belief in their potential influence their progress?

_____

_____

_____

_____

Chapter 4

SURRENDERING TO COURAGE

Courage is the choice and willingness to confront agony, pain, danger, uncertainty, or intimidation.

—Wikipedia

Embracing creativity and innovation in coaching helps clients unlock new potential and solutions while enriching the coaching experience. As coaches, let's champion the creative spirit, encouraging clients to dream, explore, and invent new possibilities for their lives.

One day, I reread something I had encountered often: "I must overcome myself before I can genuinely forgive others for injuries done to me. The self in me cannot forgive injuries." While reading this, something within me instantly made me believe these words. As a practicing coach, I can more passionately support self-forgiveness with my clients. When a client's coachable topic involves working through "self-forgiveness," I intend to inspire them to move forward. I also believe hope is sometimes transferable through emotional intelligence skills.

WHAT IS EMOTIONAL INTELLIGENCE?

Emotional intelligence is the ability to perceive, reason with, understand, and manage emotions, both within yourself and from others. It's an approach that invests time and attention in one's strengths, core values, and principled guidance rather than focusing on disorders, deficits, and character defects.

While someone's journey may not have always been easy, pretty, or comfortable—or conversely, it may have been easy, lovely, and relaxed—there comes a time when letting go of what was and reconstructing what is becomes essential. This reconstruction builds on the eight "C" qualities: curiosity, compassion, calmness, clarity (i.e., perspective), courage, confidence, creativity, and connectedness. These qualities cannot be damaged or destroyed, no matter how severe the traumatic experiences.

Building on these "C" qualities increases self-energy, emphasizes internal healing and very helpful in treating fragmented spirits. There is more to say about the spirit of not giving up. Marianne Williamson states, "Liberated from our deepest fears/ Our presence automatically liberates others" (Our Deepest Fear, Lines 27-28). This liberation is at the core of the Internal Family Systems (IFS) approach (Schwartz & Sweezy, 2020).

Courage is a fundamental trait that both coaches and clients must cultivate. As coaches, we need the courage to challenge our clients, ask difficult questions and hold space for uncomfortable emotions. We must also be courageous enough to face our limitations and biases, constantly working on our personal growth to better serve our clients.

For clients, courage often means facing their fears, stepping out of their comfort zones and embracing change. As coaches, we can help our clients develop courage by creating a safe and supportive environment where they feel empowered to take risks. We can encourage them to reframe their perception of failure, seeing it as a valuable learning opportunity rather than a setback. We reinforce this vital trait by celebrating small acts of bravery and helping clients recognize their courage.

One effective way to help clients build courage is through gradual exposure to challenging situations. We can work with clients to break down their goals into smaller, manageable steps, each requiring a bit of courage. As they successfully navigate these steps, their confidence grows, and they become more willing to face more significant challenges. Additionally, we can use visualization techniques, helping clients imagine themselves successfully overcoming obstacles, which can boost their courage when facing real-life situations. By combining these strategies with ongoing support and encouragement, we can help our clients develop the courage they need to pursue their dreams and live authentically.

THE POWER OF BOUNDARIES:
PRIORITIZING SELF IN A DEMANDING ROLE

One of the first steps in saving space for oneself is learning to set and uphold boundaries. This can be challenging, especially when you are passionate about your clients' progress and invested in their success. However, boundaries are essential for maintaining energy and protecting emotional space. Without clear boundaries, the lines between your personal and professional life blur, leaving you vulnerable to overwork and emotional exhaustion. Establishing designated times for client sessions, setting limits on availability outside those times, and protecting your time for rest and rejuvenation are all critical aspects of boundary-setting.

Boundaries also extend beyond the practical and into the emotional. As a coach, you often allow clients to share their deepest fears, frustrations, and pain. While empathy is essential in coaching, avoiding absorbing your clients' emotional states is crucial. Observing and supporting them without internalizing their struggles allows you to remain grounded in your emotional reality. To achieve this, incorporate mindfulness, energy clearing, or breathwork into your routine, ensuring you leave room for emotional renewal after intense coaching sessions.

Anger kills Wisdom
Wisdom Heals Anger

Dishonesty kills Self-Honesty
Self-Honesty Heals Dis-Honesty

Doubt kills Confidence
Confidence Heals Doubt

Ego kills Dignity
Dignity Heals Ego

Fatigue kills Progress
Progress Heals Fatigue

Doubt kills Faith
Faith Heals Doubt

Goals kills Dreams
Dreams Heals Goals

Hopelessness kills Hope
Hope Heals Hopelessness

Jealousy kills Peace
Peace Heals Jealously

Laziness kills Energy
Energy Heals Laziness

Misery kills Joy
Joy kills Misery

THE COACH WITHIN

Powerlessness kills Power
Power Heals Powerlessness

Fear kills Courage
Courage conquers Fear

Closed-mindedness kills Open-mindedness
Open-mindedness Heals Closed-mindedness

Depression kills Happiness
Happiness heals Depression

Anger kills Calmness
Calmness Heals Anger

Rudeness kills Gratitude
Gratitude Heals Rudeness

Self-Pity kills Self-Esteem
Self-Esteem Heals Self-Pity

Fear kills freedom
Freedom Heals Fear

Worry kills Serenity
Serenity Heals Worry

Resentment kills Love
Love Heals Resentment

Hate kills Love
Love Heals Hate

Folly Kills Character
Character Heals Folly

Stress kills Self-Awareness
Self-Awareness Heals Stress

Blame kills forgiveness
Forgiveness Heals Blame

Hate kills Love
Love Heals Hate

—Adapted by Leona P. Jackson

Transformation doesn't just happen. It takes a plan to start, a support system to progress, a strategy to follow, accomplishing measurable goals and becoming a successful client and coach.

As we close this chapter, it feels only fitting to reflect on all twelve principles, embracing their positivity now that we've surrendered the stubborn will to cling to mental injuries long after the offenses have passed. We've discovered that self-honesty opens the door to more

profound hope, strengthening our capacity for extraordinary acts of faith. Courage becomes a daily practice, integrity transforms our will, intentions, and willingness sparks unexpected shifts in our attitudes.

Resting in the spirit of love brings comfort and joy, while forgiveness is a deeply personal and liberating reward. Self-discipline shapes a new and fulfilling way of life, and self-awareness sharpens greater understanding of our motives, intentions, and actions. Finally, through the practice of service, we learn the beauty of giving and receiving, expressing gratitude for the ultimate gift giver. These principles illuminate a path toward growth, healing, and inner peace.

ACTIONABLE PRACTICE QUESTIONS

1. What small act of courage can you commit to this week that will push you outside your comfort zone?

_____

_____

_____

_____

2. Reflect on past wounds by reframing past hurts. How can you reframe it as a learning experience rather than a setback?

_____

_____

_____

_____

3. What of the "C" qualities (curiosity, compassion, calmness, clarity, courage, confidence, creativity, connectedness) resonates most with you, and how can you fully embody them?

_____

_____

_____

_____

4. Identify a boundary you need to set to protect your time or energy. What steps can you take to reinforce it?

_____

_____

_____

_____

5. Visualize yourself overcoming a current challenge. What emotions or qualities do you feel as you succeed?

_____

_____

_____

_____

Chapter 5

SURRENDERING TO INTEGRITY

Integrity—is defined as the quality of being honest and
having strong moral principles.

—Merrian/Webster

At its core, coaching is faith in action—an exchange between self, team members, groups, or two people that holds space for the known and the unknown while allowing room for growth and strength. It's about taking what we have, no matter how incomplete, and turning it into something workable. There was a time when I was on a mission, searching for somebody who could make me feel like somebody. I spent years on this "Somebody Hunting Project," only to be completely shocked when I found the person I was searching for—it was me. The answer was within me all along, quietly waiting for me to stop looking outward and start looking inward.

For a long time, I didn't know what faith was, let alone how to grow it. Faith, it seemed, it was something other people had; it wasn't for me. But over time, I've realized that a series of right actions, whether intentional or not, gradually builds a foundation of faith. Slowly, faith revealed itself in my life, not as a grand, mystical force but as a series of small steps, taken one after the other. Faith is an active tool I rely on in my daily journey. It's my brand of faith—one shaped by my experiences, choices, and the lessons life has handed me. I don't have to understand precisely where faith comes from or how it works to appreciate its presence. With every breath, I can give thanks for whatever, wherever, or whomever this faith originates.

Reading **Break All the Rules** by Marcus Buckingham and Curt Coffman was a turning point for me. It reminded me that integrity, like faith, isn't something we find outside ourselves but cultivated within. Surrendering to integrity means acknowledging that our choices and faith in action shape our lives. It's the quiet but powerful realization that we hold the key to our growth. We are the somebody we've been waiting for.

The journey of self-discovery often leads us down unexpected paths, challenging our preconceived notions about who we are and what we're capable of achieving. Realizing I was the "somebody" I had been searching for all along was liberating and daunting. It meant that the power to change my life and cultivate the principle of faith resides within me and is manufactured by some external sources or a savior.

This newfound understanding of faith as a personal, evolving force has transformed my approach to life's challenges. I've come to see that faith isn't a static quality bestowed upon the lucky few but rather a dynamic, growing aspect of our lives that we can nurture through consistent action and reflection. By embracing this perspective, I've learned to trust my abilities and intuition, allowing me to navigate life's uncertainties more confidently and resiliently. The journey of surrendering to integrity becomes about finding faith and cultivating a deep, abiding trust in oneself and the process of personal growth.

GRATITUDE FOR IMPACT: CELEBRATING THE WINS, BIG AND SMALL

Every coach knows the joy of witnessing a client's breakthrough moment. Whether it's achieving a long-term goal, overcoming a mental barrier, or having a realization that changes everything, these moments are gratifying. It's easy to feel a sense of gratitude when your clients succeed, but it's just as important to cultivate gratitude for the smaller, quieter wins. Sometimes, progress looks like a shift in mindset, the courage to take a new step, or simply showing up consistently for themselves.

By celebrating these moments of growth, you acknowledge your client's hard work and reinforce the power of incremental change. Gratitude for these small wins allows you to stay present with your clients in their day-to-day journey, not just at the finish line. It also teaches your clients the value of appreciating their progress and helps them stay motivated, even when the path forward seems slow. Gratitude, in this sense, becomes a practice of recognizing and honoring growth in all its forms.

Managing stress is crucial for sustaining high performance over the long term. By implementing strategic stress management techniques, high performers can protect our health and continue to excel in coaching endeavors. As coaches, we provide the tools and support to navigate these challenges effectively.

Also, when used wisely, technology can be a powerful ally in personal developmental journeys. It offers endless resources and tools to tailor our growth paths with better accessibility, accountability, and applications, making learning and improvement more reliable.

As we close this chapter, it feels only fitting to reflect on all twelve principles, embracing their positivity now that we've surrendered the stubborn will to cling to mental injuries long after the offenses have passed. We've discovered that self-honesty opens the door to more profound hope, strengthening our capacity for extraordinary acts of faith. Courage becomes a daily practice, integrity transforms our will, intentions, and willingness sparks unexpected shifts in our attitudes.

Resting in the spirit of love brings comfort and joy, while forgiveness is a deeply personal and liberating reward. Self-discipline shapes a new and fulfilling way of life, and self-awareness sharpens greater understanding of our motives, intentions, and actions. Finally, through the practice of service, we learn the beauty of giving and receiving, expressing gratitude for the ultimate gift giver. These principles illuminate a path toward growth, healing, and inner peace.

ACTIONABLE PRACTICE QUESTIONS

1. Reflect on a time you searched for validation outside yourself. How can you turn inward for that sense of value?

_____

_____

_____

_____

2. What small steps can you take today to strengthen your faith in yourself and your journey?

_____

_____

_____

_____

3. Identify one area where you can act with greater integrity. What change will you make?

_____

_____

_____

_____

4. Recall a recent "small win" you achieved. How did it impact your journey, and how can you celebrate it?

_____

_____

_____

_____

5. List one stress management technique you can implement to support your growth and resilience.

_____

_____

_____

_____

Chapter 6

SURRENDERING TO WILLINGNESS

Willingness-The quality or state of being
prepared to do something; readiness:
—Oxford Advanced
Learner's Dictionary

I unknowingly needed a coach long before I realized it. The idea of surrendering to willingness—to being open to growth, change, and guidance—eluded me for much of my life. Does the hope of a coach transfer to the hope of a client? Sometimes, it does, but what truly makes the difference is the client's willingness to accept that hope and transform it into action. My willingness to truly live, not just survive, became part of an internal system that extended beyond financial success was woven into how I approached friendships, cared for myself, and connected to my purpose.

On August 2, 2024, I had the privilege of speaking at a conference. As I stood there, sharing my experience, strength, and hope with others,

I felt no fear—only gratitude. It became clear to me that my faith had made me whole. In that moment, I understood the beauty of the creative process, the grace to grow, heal, and help others. I finally embraced faith, courage, and the willingness to engage with life and its many lessons fully. Self-honesty, humility, love, and perseverance were no longer abstract concepts. They were living, breathing parts of me.

Principle living shaped my journey and prepared me to guide others. Through my forty-seven years of growth, I've understood that coaching is a partnership. Both the coach and the client have assignments, each with responsibilities. As a coach, I guide, support, and provide structure, but the real work lies within the clients willingness to engage, change, and grow. First, I'll try to speak to the client's assignment.

The client must be:

1.   Surrendered to the fact that change is needed.

2.   Ready or at least willing to begin the process of change.

3.   Prepared to set achievable goals.

4.   Bold in creating, engaging, and completing assignments.

5. Willing to ask, share, and study.

6. Able to create assignments to move forward.

7. Have an idea of what growth looks like for them.

8. Know, articulate, and assimilate stages of growth.

9. Tell their life story in relatable sections.

10. Tell their leadership story.

11. Encourage notetaking daily.

12. Practice coaching your external coach when possible.

13. Go deep and add value.

14. Establish credibility.

15. Understand their agenda.

16. Build rapport.

The journey of surrendering to willingness is a transformative process that often begins with the realization that change is necessary and will become more desirable with time. It's a profound shift in mindset, where resistance gives way to acceptance, and fear of the unknown is replaced by curiosity and openness. This willingness becomes the fertile ground for personal growth and development to flourish.

In my experience, the path to willingness was not a straight line. It was fraught with detours, setbacks, and moments of self-doubt. However, each challenge taught me valuable lessons about resilience, adaptability, and the power of perseverance. The turning point came when I realized that willingness was not about relinquishing control but rather about embracing the possibilities that change could bring.

A coach-client relationship is a delicate dance of trust, vulnerability, and shared commitment to growth. As a client, one must be willing to expose one's strengths, weaknesses, and fears. This level of openness can be daunting, but it's essential for meaningful progress. The coach, in turn, must create a safe space for this vulnerability, offering guidance without judgment and challenges without criticism.

Ultimately, surrendering willingness is about more than personal growth—discovering one's authentic self and purpose. It fosters peeling away layers of societal expectations, self-imposed limitations, and past experiences that may have clouded our vision of who we are and what we're capable of achieving. Through this process, we transform ourselves and gain the ability to positively impact those around us, creating a ripple effect of growth and positive change in our communities and beyond.

Lastly, "coaching your coach" introduces an interesting dynamic to the coaching relationship. It suggests a level of engagement and reciprocity beyond the traditional coach-client hierarchy. By encouraging clients to participate in the coaching process actively, we foster a more collaborative and mutually beneficial relationship with both parties continuously learning and growing together.

COACH LEONA'S STORY

I was born and raised in Kansas City, Missouri, on January 4, 1947. My mother claimed she delivered me herself, a one-sentence story she casually shared when I was in my early thirties. I find it hard to believe, but back then, life was often complex, cruel, and brutal, so perhaps it was or wasn't true. I do not know. My childhood was filled with fear of people, places, and things that seemed to haunt me non-stop into adulthood.

When I grew up, I traveled a lot, from Kansas City, Missouri, to Kansas City, Kansas; Albuquerque, New Mexico; Lubbock, Texas; and Seattle, Washington. Emotional trauma became my unhealthy coping mechanism, my constant fellow traveler, and my ride-or-die enemy. By 1972, I found myself unknowingly exhausted by a fixed mindset, unhealthy coping skills, and seemingly inability to want any part of the ideal of change. The willingness to change brought a bleak surrender to the unthinkable stronghold of not changing. But I was unsure where or how to begin the wanting, needing, or consideration of embracing change.

I enrolled in my first typing class that year or the next, hoping it would be a small step toward something better. One day, after class, I noticed a small purple and black brochure in the lobby of the vocational building. It caught my eye. The front read: CALL THIS NUMBER: Need Education? Need Food? Need Shelter? Need Clothing? Need Training? But it was the last line that shook me: NEED MENTAL HELP? Call this Number. I was curious; something inside me stirred as I opened the brochure to the page and read the black print.

Trying to figure out what spun me into dedicated action that day was all emotionally driven. I only remember that something resonated with me on the page. The fine print on the page spoke to my deepest, unspoken, pitiful, and incomprehensible demoralization and fears. I hurried home. Suddenly, the situation had become an emergency within my chaotic mind space. As I dashed through the door, I picked up the phone and dialed the number given; after a while, I asked the receptionist if I needed an appointment. The receptionist suggested that I come right on in. I delivered my two kids to a babysitter and sped to what seemed like intensive care.

I drove straight to my first wellness clinic. At the time, I considered myself a social drinker. But by 1977, five years after that fateful first wellness clinic visit, I had become a full-blown, hope-to-die obsessive drinker. I drank to forget. I drank to keep myself from thinking about that trips to the wellness clinic. I couldn't figure out why I had checked myself in, in the first place, I wasn't that bad, I kept telling myself, but deep down, I knew the truth—I was worse than I could comprehend or admit. The drinking was just another symptom of the fear, the trauma, and the unworthiness that had followed me since childhood. Although it wasn't drinking yet; it was my ratchet radical thinking.

That moment with the brochure helped me step toward seeking help and marked the beginning of a long, mighty journey. It would take decades to understand what surrendering to change genuinely meant that day, but that initial willingness to ask for help started by picking up the purple and black brochure over five decades ago.

As we close this chapter, it feels only fitting to reflect on all twelve principles, embracing their positivity now that we've surrendered the stubborn will to cling to mental injuries long after the offenses have passed. We've discovered that self-honesty opens the door to more profound hope, strengthening our capacity for extraordinary acts of faith. Courage becomes a daily practice, integrity transforms our will, intentions, and willingness sparks unexpected shifts in our attitudes.

Resting in the spirit of love brings comfort and joy, while forgiveness is a deeply personal and liberating reward. Self-discipline shapes a new and fulfilling way of life, and self-awareness sharpens greater understanding of our motives, intentions, and actions. Finally, through the practice of service, we learn the beauty of giving and receiving, expressing gratitude for the ultimate gift giver. These principles illuminate a path toward growth, healing, and inner peace.

ACTIONABLE PRACTICE QUESTIONS

1. What change are you currently resisting, and how could a willingness to embrace it open new possibilities?

_____

_____

_____

_____

2. Reflect on a time you took a small step toward change. What motivated you, and what did you learn?

_____

_____

_____

_____

3. Identify one area where you can be more open to guidance or support. How might this willingness impact your growth?

_____

_____

_____

_____

4. Think of a habit or mindset holding you back. What small action can you take today to move toward positive change?

_____

_____

_____

_____

5. What strengths or values can you lean on to support your journey toward greater willingness and openness?

_____

_____

_____

_____

Chapter 7

SURRENDERING TO HUMILITY

Humility (noon): The quality of having a modest
view of one's value or importance.
—Oxford English Dictionary

Humility (verb): A rising in spirit
—Anonymous

Coaching moved me from numbness to a life rooted in self-worth. I'll never forget a pivotal moment in my journey when I felt utterly lost, pacing the floor of a meeting hall, mumbling to myself, unsure of what weighed so heavily on my heart. A young man passing by overheard me and said, *"Leona, you're feeling unworthy!"* His words struck me like a bolt of lightning. I hadn't even realized that I was struggling with worthiness versus unworthiness—it had such a firm grip on me, yet I was oblivious to it. That day reminded me of the saying, "the darkest hour just before dawn." However, at that moment, I knew he was right. Something shifted within me immediately. Whether it was a small or large shift, I can't say, but I felt a healing begin. It was as if, I started to understand what it meant to embody worthiness.

God's grace met me there, more than enough for that day and every day since. Surrendering to both the known and the unknown has become part of my daily practice—a process I approach with humility. Wes Moore once said, *"Tutelage moves us from a place of numbness to hope and well-being. From bondage to freedom and hangs us in the balance of every action we take."* Reflecting on this, I see how surrendering to self-honesty, faith, and hope, during distress, became a lifeline.

Humility has been the key to transforming feelings of bondage into freedom again and again. Every step forward feels like a tribute, evidence, and grace surrounding me. The more I embrace my authentic self, the more life flows into me, restoring me piece by piece. As I sit here typing, I marveled at how thoughts form into sentences, how sentences convey complete ideas—how words, seemingly simple and disconnected, come together to express something deep and real. This fluidity exists in the coaching relationship, too. I wondered which is more valuable: the questions or the answers? Now I see that both are equally essential—like ying and yang, partners in the journey of discovery.

In coaching, as in life, humility invites us to surrender to the process, allowing questions and answers to guide our growth and transformation.

"Where would I be if it had not been for the Lord on my side?"
Psalm 124:1 (NKJV)

The journey of surrendering to humility is often marked by moments of profound realization, much like my experience in wellness opportunities. These epiphanies can come from unexpected sources, reminding us that wisdom and insight can be found in the most unlikely places. The young man's observation about unworthiness struck a chord, highlighting how sometimes we need an external perspective to illuminate our internal struggles.

This process of self-discovery through humility is only sometimes comfortable. It requires us to confront our vulnerabilities and acknowledge our limitations. However, we often find our most excellent growth opportunities through this very discomfort. By embracing humility, we open ourselves to new perspectives and possibilities we might have overlooked.

The transformation from numbness to self-worthiness is a testament to the power of coaching and self-reflection. This journey involves peeling back layers of self-doubt and societal conditioning to reveal our true, worthy selves. It's a process of self-discovery and revitalization, unearthing the inherent value that has always been present but perhaps obscured by life's challenges and our self-limiting beliefs.

Accepting the known and unknown is crucial to surrendering to humility. It requires us to acknowledge that we don't have all the answers and that there is always more to learn. This mindset fosters a sense of curiosity and openness that can lead to continuous personal growth and development.

The reflection on the writing process beautifully illustrates the interplay between conscious thought and subconscious creativity. This observation is a metaphor for the coaching process, where questions and answers work together to uncover deeper truths and insights. As words flow onto the page to form coherent thoughts, our experiences and reflections coalesce into personal growth and self-understanding through the coaching journey.

Lastly, comparing questions and answers to ying and yang underscores the holistic nature of personal development. Like these complementary forces in Chinese philosophy, questions and answers in coaching are interconnected and interdependent. They create a dynamic balance that propels us forward on our journey of self-discovery and growth. This balance reminds us that surrendering to humility means not diminishing ourselves but opening ourselves to our full potential.

THE PRACTICE OF SELF-REFLECTION: NURTURING YOUR PERSONAL GROWTH

Just as you encourage your clients to engage in self-reflection, it is equally essential for you as a coach. Saving space for yourself means creating time to reflect on your emotional and personal growth. Take time to check in with yourself regularly—assess where you are emotionally, mentally, and spiritually. What lessons are unfolding in your life? How are you growing and evolving in your coaching practice? These reflective moments clarify and ensure that you remain aligned with your purpose and values as a coach.

Self-reflection can take many forms. Journaling is a powerful tool for unpacking emotions, challenges, and successes. Writing down your thoughts and feelings can bring clarity and insight into areas where you need to set boundaries or give yourself more care. Additionally, regular reflection helps you avoid burnout by addressing minor stressors before they become overwhelming. Meditation, silence, and time spent in nature are other effective ways to create stillness and check in with yourself. In this space, you can reconnect with your inner wisdom, listen to your needs, and honor your evolution.

As we close this chapter, it feels only fitting to reflect on all twelve principles, embracing their positivity now that we've surrendered the stubborn will to cling to mental injuries long after the offenses have passed. We've discovered that self-honesty opens the door to more profound hope, strengthening our capacity for extraordinary acts of faith. Courage becomes a daily practice, integrity transforms our will, intentions, and willingness sparks unexpected shifts in our attitudes.

Resting in the spirit of love brings comfort and joy, while forgiveness is a deeply personal and liberating reward. Self-discipline shapes a new and fulfilling way of life, and self-awareness sharpens greater understanding of our motives, intentions, and actions. Finally, through the practice of service, we learn the beauty of giving and receiving, expressing gratitude for the ultimate gift giver. These principles illuminate a path toward growth, healing, and inner peace.

ACTIONABLE PRACTICE QUESTIONS

1. Reflect on a recent moment when you felt unworthy. How can you practice seeing your intrinsic worth in such moments?

_____

_____

_____

_____

2. When has humility allowed you to learn from an unexpected source? What did you gain from this experience?

_____

_____

_____

_____

3. Identify an area where you feel resistant to humility. How might embracing humility open you to growth there?

_____

_____

_____

_____

4. How does self-reflection currently fit into your life? What can you add to make this practice more intentional?

_____

_____

_____

_____

5. Reflect on a time when you struggled with having all the answers. How can you surrender to the unknown with curiosity?

_____

_____

_____

_____

Chapter 8

SURRENDERING TO LOVE

Love is a bond forged in spirit and inner truth of authenticity and
strengthened by dedication, devotion and emotional behaviors
characterized by passion, warmth, and commitment
—Leona P. Jackson

One of the most essential skills for a coach is the ability to transform ordinary interactions into meaningful dialogues. As coaches, we must communicate effectively, guide clients, and model behaviors that foster leadership and success.

"Perfection is not attainable, but if we chase perfection, we can catch excellence."

—Vince Lombardi.

This quote encapsulates the coaching spirit, encouraging us to add balance, depth, and weight to our work while helping clients understand the known and unknown. As coaches, we strive to create a client space to gain clarity and insight in a timely and authentic manner. The relationship I admire most is the one I've developed with myself over the past 47 years. I've finally found the confidence to standalone without feeling the aloneness,' self-sufficient without being selfish, and hunger without being obsessive. A sense of balance and well-being has emerged from the core of my being—my soul's anchor—and caring for it has become a source of joy.

I've learned to meet my needs without relying on temporary crutches like compulsions, overeating, drinking, gambling, excessive talking, smoking, blaming, or complaining. I hold myself accountable when I stumble, fall, or fail, just as I do when I succeed, climb out of life's rabbit holes and stand firmly in my integrity. Improving my life is a continuous journey. My emotional companions are the 8 "C's"— Calmness, Curiosity, Compassion, Clarity, Creativity, Courage, Confidence, and Connectedness.

Time management for me isn't just about cramming more into each day. It's about using the right tools at the right time. As coaches, one of our challenges is helping clients develop the ability to make conscious choices about their most precious resource: time. Who do I say I am? This is a crucial question to explore. As coaches, we listen deeply and ask the questions that will lead to a defining "aha" moment for both the client and ourselves. The journey of surrendering to love begins with self-acceptance and then radiates outward, embracing others with authenticity and compassion. This transformation process asks us to acknowledge vulnerabilities while celebrating our strengths, laying a foundation for personal growth and meaningful connections. Through surrender, we discover that love is more than just an emotion; it's a powerful force shaping our interactions, decisions, and life paths.

Self-sufficiency, balanced with interconnectedness, reflects a mature understanding of love's dual nature. While we must cultivate inner strength and self-reliance, we must maintain open hearts and minds, ready to give and receive love. This paradox creates a dynamic tension that fosters growth and deepens our ability to form meaningful relationships.

In the coaching relationship, love is reflected in deep listening, genuine curiosity, and unwavering support for the client's journey. The role of a coach isn't to fix or change the client but to provide a safe space where self-discovery and transformation can unfold. This requires patience, wisdom, and the ability to hold space for struggles and successes, all while maintaining professional boundaries. Integrating time management with personal development emphasizes the practical side of self-love. Helping clients make conscious choices about spending their time and energy shows that love includes respecting our limitations and honoring our needs. This blend of practical wisdom and emotional intelligence forms the foundation for personal and professional growth that is both sustainable and deeply fulfilling.

As we close this chapter, it feels only fitting to reflect on all twelve principles, embracing their positivity now that we've surrendered the stubborn will to cling to mental injuries long after the offenses have passed. We've discovered that self-honesty opens the door to more profound hope, strengthening our capacity for extraordinary acts of faith. Courage becomes a daily practice, integrity transforms our will, intentions, and willingness sparks unexpected shifts in our attitudes.

Resting in the spirit of love brings comfort and joy, while forgiveness is a deeply personal and liberating reward. Self-discipline shapes a new and fulfilling way of life, and self-awareness sharpens greater understanding of our motives, intentions, and actions. Finally, through the practice of service, we learn the beauty of giving and receiving, expressing gratitude for the ultimate gift giver. These principles illuminate a path toward growth, healing, and inner peace.

ACTIONABLE PRACTICE QUESTIONS

1. Reflect on how you currently balance self-sufficiency with openness to others. What steps can you take to enhance both?

_____

_____

_____

_____

2. When was the last time you held space for someone without trying to solve their problem? How did it feel, and what did you learn?

_____

_____

_____

_____

3. Identify one area where you can apply more compassion toward yourself. How might this influence your relationships with others?

_____

_____

_____

_____

4. What small, conscious choice can you make today to manage your time in a way that honors your needs?

_____

_____

_____

_____

5. Reflect on your current definition of self-love. How does it shape your actions and decisions?

_____

_____

_____

_____

Chapter 9

SELF-DISCIPLINE

Self-Discipline—The ability to control one's feelings and
overcome one's weaknesses; the ability to pursue what
one thinks is right despite temptations to abandon it.
—Oxford English Dictionary

I had only been practicing this new way of life for about a week, but something about the laughter, the seriousness, and the preamble read at the start of each session inspired me to keep returning. Based on past patterns and inability to stay consistent, I knew I would likely fall off the map eventually. That was forty-seven years, four months, and eighteen days ago.

It was a Sunday morning, and I must have arrived early. I found, My self, standing on the porch of the facility, pacing back and forth, Impatiently, frantically, and anxiously waiting for other members and guests to arrive. Suddenly, this question popped into my mind: How will they know I haven't taken a drink? My intuition answered, *you will know*. For whatever reason, I understood the depth of that response over forty-seven years ago.

At some point that same day, or perhaps on another occasion, I stood on that same porch, watching the Sunday churchgoers driving past. A thought entered my mind: Could it be possible that all the churchgoers are right, and I am wrong? There was no immediate answer, just silence. But for the first time, I admitted to myself that I could be wrong. Within that moment, I felt a strange sense of comfort— what I now recognized as a feeling of humility. At the time, I had no idea what was happening inside my mind or brain, but I knew something was shifting, something working in my favor. I was finally ready to let go of the obsession with what others thought of me.

"I've learned that if a person is willing to look at another person's behavior toward them as a reflection of the state of their relationship with themselves, rather than as a statement about their value as a person, then you will, over time, cease to react at all to their reactions toward you."

THE FOUR AGREEMENTS: A PRACTICAL GUIDE TO PERSONAL FREEDOM BY DON MIGUEL RUIZ.

This journey of surrendering to self-discipline begins with small but profound moments of clarity, like my experience on that porch. These moments, while seemingly insignificant, are the foundation for lasting change. The power is not in the magnitude of the moment but in the willingness to be open to these subtle shifts that can transform our worldview over time.

Self-discipline is often misunderstood. It's not merely about restriction or control. Instead, it's about creating space for growth and understanding through consistency and patient self-observation. The realization that you will know highlights a fundamental truth: authentic self-discipline is an internal process guided by an innate compass rather than external validation. As we surrender old thinking patterns and behavior, this internal compass becomes sharper and more dependable.

Developing self-discipline requires us to acknowledge limitations and embrace the discomfort of not knowing everything. When we stand in that uneasy space between what we've always believed and what might be true, we open ourselves to a more profound personal transformation. My moment of questioning whether I was wrong to the churchgoers illustrates this beautifully. In these humbling moments, when we allow ourselves to doubt our certainty, we break free from our rigid thinking and open the door to growth and new possibilities.

Deliver me from the traps of self-deception, embrace the truth of self-honesty and let me understand that the only real victim of self-dishonesty here is myself.

As we close this chapter, it feels only fitting to reflect on all twelve principles, embracing their positivity now that we've surrendered the stubborn will to cling to mental injuries long after the offenses have passed. We've discovered that self-honesty opens the door to more

profound hope, strengthening our capacity for extraordinary acts of faith. Courage becomes a daily practice, integrity transforms our will, intentions, and willingness sparks unexpected shifts in our attitudes.

Resting in the spirit of love brings comfort and joy, while forgiveness is a deeply personal and liberating reward. Self-discipline shapes a new and fulfilling way of life, and self-awareness sharpens greater understanding of our motives, intentions, and actions. Finally, through the practice of service, we learn the beauty of giving and receiving, expressing gratitude for the ultimate gift giver. These principles illuminate a path toward growth, healing, and inner peace.

ACTIONABLE PRACTICE QUESTIONS

1. Reflect on a past mistake you've struggled to forgive. What would self-forgiveness look like in this situation?

_____

_____

_____

_____

2. Recall a moment when you felt by your standards rather than others. How did that impact your self-discipline?

_____

_____

_____

_____

3. Identify a limiting belief you hold about yourself. How might questioning it open up new possibilities?

_____

_____

_____

_____

4. Think of an area where you've been hard on yourself. What steps can you take today to show yourself compassion?

_____

_____

_____

_____

5. How can you cultivate more self-honesty in your daily life? What practice will help sharpen your internal compass?

_____

_____

_____

_____

Chapter 10

SURRENDERING TO PERSEVERANCE

Perseverance is the continued effort to do or achieve
something despite difficulties, failure, or opposition.

—Merriam/Webster

I am still uncovering the most exciting and essential truths about
myself. After enduring trauma from the ages of six to sixteen, the
emotional residue left me numb, sleepwalking through life, and often
vicious during my teens, twenties, thirties, forties, fifties, and sixties.
It wasn't until my seventies that my body, mind, and soul truly
awakened, allowing me to function better. Then, I began to speak my
truth, something I didn't even know was possible in my younger years.

At thirty, I surrendered to not drinking—one day at a time, but I
remained emotionally crippled. It wasn't until I reached thirty-five that
I could genuinely smile and laugh—an exhilarating discovery. By

turning forty, I had earned the gift of self-forgiveness. And by forgiving myself, I could forgive those who had damaged my path, understanding that they, too, were incapable of loving themselves, let alone me. As I grew spiritually and naturally, I shifted from an "I can't" mentality to "I can do better."

Writing became a tool of liberation, relieving me of the self-hate and shame that had once shackled me. Slowly but surely, I learned to love life and myself—a revelation that still amazes me today. I can boldly say that I love myself—and that self-love is one of the most exciting deliverables I've experienced.

I'm starting my own coaching business, and who I've become is one of the most thrilling revelations I can announce today. I am free from so many things that once held me captive: broken heart syndrome, chronic stress, emotional stress, nightmare disorder, denial, hyperactivity, compulsive gambling, nicotine addiction, anger outbursts, mood swings, poor planning, insomnia, alcohol addiction, debt, shame, loneliness, guilt, and the endless search for Mr. Right. Today, I am also free from blaming, criticizing, finding fault, and the self-pity that kept me in bondage from six to seventy years old, on some level or another. Thank God! Now I understand that each day brings two choices: a "chance to change" and a "choice to make." Signed: I choose—for with that choice, and through God's power, I find the strength to persevere.

The journey of perseverance, as described, highlights an essential truth: it appears that healing and growth follows their own unique timelines. This story is powerful not because of the transformation itself but because of the patience accepted at each stage of development. Each decade seems to have brought additional revelations and victories, no matter how small or large. Perseverance isn't about rushing toward a goal but maintaining steady forward movement, even when progress feels slow or invisible.

The author's narrative of freedom from various addictions and emotional barriers demonstrates that perseverance is not a straight path but rather a complex, evolving journey. Every victory—whether breaking free from substance abuse, unhealthy emotional patterns, or destructive behaviors—became a building block for sustaining growth.

Perseverance is small and large, consistent choices to change, ultimately leading to profound life changes, even after many years of struggle. The culmination of this journey in the decision to become a coach speaks volumes about the power of perseverance. By turning personal struggles into a force for helping others, the author shows how perseverance can evolve from being a survival mechanism to a way of serving others. This transformation from surviving to thriving demonstrates how perseverance leads to personal healing and equips us to contribute to the journeys of others —meaningfully.

As we close this chapter, it feels only fitting to reflect on all twelve principles, embracing their positivity now that we've surrendered the stubborn will to cling to mental injuries long after the offenses have passed. We've discovered that self-honesty opens the door to more

profound hope, strengthening our capacity for extraordinary acts of faith. Courage becomes a daily practice, integrity transforms our will, intentions, and willingness sparks unexpected shifts in our attitudes.

Resting in the spirit of love brings comfort and joy, while forgiveness is a deeply personal and liberating reward. Self-discipline shapes a new and fulfilling way of life, and self-awareness sharpens greater understanding of our motives, intentions, and actions. Finally, through the practice of service, we learn the beauty of giving and receiving, expressing gratitude for the ultimate gift giver. These principles illuminate a path toward growth, healing, and inner peace.

ACTIONABLE PRACTICE QUESTIONS

1. Identify an area of your life where self-discipline is lacking. What small steps can you take today to build consistency in that area?

_____

_____

_____

_____

2. Reflect on a past habit or behavior you overcame. What lessons from that experience can you apply to current challenges?

_____

_____

_____

_____

3. When faced with a setback, how can you persevere rather than give up?

_____

_____

_____

_____

4. What daily choice can you make that significantly reinforces your commitment to personal growth?

_____

_____

_____

_____

5. How can you use self-discipline to transform a current struggle into a strength?

_____

_____

_____

_____

Chapter 11

SURRENDERING TO AWARENESS

Self-Awareness is the awareness of one's own
personality or individuality.

—Merriam-Webster

"We know what we are but not what we may become."
—William Shakespeare

Change is at the heart of the coaching journey, and this year, I celebrated forty-seven years of sobriety with a symbolic gesture: I gave myself forty-seven gifts. Each present was chosen thoughtfully, lovingly, and painstakingly. The counting, wrapping and unwrapping each gift over the following months became another powerful experience. Whenever I opened a gift; it reminded me of a moment when my mind and spirit had come together in clarity, choosing something sentimental and daringly meaningful for my present and future self.

These gifts weren't merely tangible items. They were personal rewards—inner acknowledgments of growth and perseverance. Gifts to oneself are vital affirmations, small tokens of self-recognition. Many of us devote more care and attention to others, often unconsciously than ourselves. Over time, this imbalance can lead to deep resentments, first buried beneath the surface, then rising into conscious awareness. We may begin to feel a gnawing sense of shame, a discomfort we don't want to admit fully. But in those moments, it's crucial to remember that healing is a process that unfolds slowly and often unevenly.

My journey toward awareness has been moving from ignorance to determination, from reacting to the challenges around me to becoming proactive about my growth. Through this newfound awareness, I've stopped focusing so much on the problems at work, church, home, or my internal uneasiness. Instead, I've begun to honor my complications, adversities, worries, dilemmas, messes, faults, compliments, attempts, and incomplete stages of recovery and growth opportunities. Each step forward is evidence of self-honesty, hope, faith, perseverance, and other principles in action.

> *"I am learning that self-leadership is not about titles, positions, or flowcharts; it's regarding one life influencing another."*
>
> —John C. Maxwell

> *(And sometimes one's self, influencing self).*
>
> —Adapted by Leona P. Jackson

Surrendering to awareness begins with accepting our present state while remaining open to the infinite possibilities of who we might become. This delicate dance between acceptance and aspiration forms the foundation for meaningful growth. Just as my forty-seven gifts symbolize each year of sobriety, awareness itself is a gift—a continuous process of unwrapping new layers of understanding, one GIFT at a time. Self-awareness is more than just observing our actions; it's about Exploring our motivations of hope, faith, beliefs, and other healing patterns that drive our actions into a place of total surrendering peace and happiness.

It's recognizing when we're operating from old, outdated scripts and consciously deciding to rewrite new scripts to practice. Once we become more aware of our faulty patterns, we begin to see how past experiences have shaped us, and we can gain the power to reshape our future beyond those influences.

A fundamental shift in this journey is moving from problem-focused thinking to solution-oriented awareness. It's not that life's problems disappear, but our relationship with them transforms. We begin to see obstacles not as insurmountable barriers but as opportunities for growth. This shift in perspective is perhaps one of the greatest gifts that heightened awareness brings.

In professional and personal growth, self-awareness acts like a lighthouse, shining its beam on both the safe paths and the dangerous waters. It helps us navigate the complexities of our emotions, relationships, and inner growth with greater clarity and purpose. As we give ourselves both literal and metaphorical gifts, we reinforce this awareness, acknowledging the strides we've made and the progress to come.

Awareness and healing are intimately linked. We can pause before reacting as we become more conscious of our behaviors, triggers, and responses. This pause creates the space for deliberate, thoughtful actions aligned with our valid values. In this space, healing unfolds naturally as we address old wounds with compassion and new insight. Ultimately, the journey from focusing on problems to honoring mature efforts of awareness. It acknowledges that challenges are a natural part of life, but our responses to them shape who we become. By recognizing our growth, celebrating our wins, and respecting our struggles, we create a balanced, sustainable approach to self-development and healing.

Surrendering to awareness isn't a one-time event; it's continual practice that invites us to stay present, keep growing, and remain open to endless possibilities.

As we close this chapter, it feels only fitting to reflect on all twelve principles, embracing their positivity now that we've surrendered stubborn will to cling to mental injuries long after the offenses have passed. We've discovered that self-honesty opens the door to more profound hope, strengthening our capacity for extraordinary acts of faith. Courage becomes a daily practice, integrity transforms our will, intentions, and willingness sparks unexpected shifts in our attitudes.

Resting in the spirit of love brings comfort and joy, while forgiveness is a deeply personal and liberating reward. Self-discipline shapes a new and fulfilling way of life, and our self-awareness sharpens the understanding of our motives, intentions, and actions. Finally, through the practice of service, we learn the beauty of giving and receiving, expressing gratitude for the ultimate gift giver. These principles illuminate a path toward growth, healing, and inner peace.

ACTIONABLE PRACTICE QUESTIONS

1. Reflect on a recent challenge. What motivations or patterns do you notice in responding, and how could awareness guide you toward a different outcome?

_____

_____

_____

_____

2. Think of a time you operated on "old scripts." How might rewriting these scripts impact your growth?

_____

_____

_____

_____

3. Identify one recurring problem in your life. How can you shift from focusing on the problem to finding a solution?

_____

_____

_____

_____

4. When was the last time you acknowledged your progress or celebrated a win? What can you do today to recognize your growth?

_____

_____

_____

_____

5. How can you practice pausing before reacting in situations that trigger you? What might this space for reflection offer?

_____

_____

_____

_____

Chapter 12

SURRENDERING TO SERVICE

"Today, I know that service is doing for self and others—It is serving with an open heart and mind. It is also guided by grace, compassion, empathy, and the willingness to serve and be served."

—Leona P. Jackson

In the end, patience is a skill that enriches the entire healing process, moving us consistently past life's rough edges each day. Everyday challenges and interactions reveal the depth of our growth, allowing us to persevere through difficult trials and emerge stronger. Service work becomes a practice that refines our craft and character, filling our days with vitality and rhythm while fostering determination and motivation. Service allows me to participate in the whole scheme of life. Through serving others, I have found a way to thrive—not despite the challenges, but because of them.

Surrendering was a long process of outdated practices and useless ingrained memories were difficult to let go. The misinterpreted vibes and the misdirected sense of settling for discomfort, because true comfort felt unreachable, and kept me bound for far too long. Yet, when I finally let go, I found that service to others became vital to unlocking the keys to emotional intelligence.

Feeling the simple sensation of an open mind shifted everything, leading me to a life worth living and, more importantly, loving. As I grew in self-awareness, my coaching skills emerged to a level I never imagined possible. The power of failure, once central to my being, started to lose its grip. Instead, I filled my heart and mind with self-honesty, hope, faith, and the small victories of each new day. No longer mired in the fixed mindset that had ruled my adult life, I began to live more authentically. I learned that failing wasn't the end; it was just a step in my journey toward success.

Once, I believed that complimenting myself was taboo. I was taught that humility meant downplaying my achievements and never allowing myself to stand in the spotlight. But when I turned thirty, I realized that self-recognition was not only permissible but essential for my growth. I began acknowledging my worth. I can look at myself in the mirror and keep my eyes open now! This act of giving required courage.

I was terrified of leadership roles, including that of a single parent. Raising my children alone was one of the most challenging undertakings of my life, but I now see it as my first actual position of service. There were days when I felt like I was failing, but in retrospect, I realized parenting was on-the-job training at its best. I was teaching, learning, and leading by example. Serving my children meant giving of myself in ways that weren't always easy, but through that service, I grew stronger and more capable. Every day, I choose to show up, even when I didn't feel like I had the strength to do so, and that was a powerful act of service.

At some point, I was awakened with a deeper yearning to understand my life's purpose and the meaning behind my life's journey. Initially, I didn't have the language or understanding to fully grasp what that meant. In search of answers, I ventured into business ownership, thinking that perhaps success would provide the clarity I sought. However, that path proved to be the wrong fit. Redirecting my energy, I returned to school, eventually earning a certificate and a bachelor's degree. Though proud of these achievements, I still felt something was missing. It wasn't until I fully embraced service as a core element of my purpose that everything began to make sense.

As we close this chapter, it feels only fitting to reflect on all twelve principles, embracing their positivity now that we've surrendered the stubborn will to cling to mental injuries long after the offenses have passed. We've discovered that self-honesty opens the door to more profound hope, strengthening our capacity for extraordinary acts of faith. Courage becomes a daily practice, integrity transforms our will, intentions, and willingness sparks unexpected shifts in our attitudes.

Resting in the spirit of love brings comfort and joy, while forgiveness is a deeply personal and liberating reward. Self-discipline shapes a new and fulfilling way of life, and self-awareness sharpens greater understanding of our motives, intentions, and actions. Finally, through the practice of service, we learn the beauty of giving and receiving, expressing gratitude for the ultimate gift giver. These principles illuminate a path toward growth, healing, and inner peace.

ACTIONABLE PRACTICE QUESTIONS

1. Reflect on a recent way you've helped someone. How did this act of service impact both you and the other person?

_____

_____

_____

_____

2. Identify an area in your life where you could serve more intentionally. What small step can you take today?

_____

_____

_____

_____

3. When did you last acknowledge your achievements? How might celebrating these moments encourage you to serve others?

_____

_____

_____

_____

4. Think of a role or responsibility that challenged you. How did it shape your understanding of service and leadership?

_____

_____

_____

_____

5. How can you integrate compassion and empathy more fully into your daily interactions?

_____

_____

_____

_____

CULTIVATING A SENSE OF UNCONDITIONAL SELF-WORTH

WISDOM AND WISENESS

1	Self-honesty	Be true to self—Surrender—Power
2	Hope	Belief in a power greater than self (An inner, peaceful strength)
3	Faith	Freedom from self-will—reliance on inner peace, strength, and fortitude
4	Courage	Fearless appraisal of ourselves (An inner source)
5	Integrity	Admission to righteousness—our true, uplifting self
6	Willingness	A speedy contribution towards release, deliverance, and assurance.
7	Humility	A rising capacity of spirit
8	Love	Mental, Spiritual, and Physical Leadership (Relationship reviews)
9	Forgiveness	A choice of restoration of self-mending.

10	Perseverance	Daily mind, body, and soul mending
11	Awareness	Spiritual Awareness—Self Awareness
12	Service	Gratitude, Serenity, and humility in the face of each challenge.
13	The Light	Light is not on you; it has got to be within you!
14	A Stand	"I am not new to this, but I'm true to this"!
15	Stuck	Save yourself from going too far down daily unnecessary rabbit holes of life.
16	Folly	Joy to those without wisdom (Wisdom-less)!
17	Self-Support	Check yourself before you wreck yourself!
18	Self-sabotage	Actions taken before thoroughly investigating the consequences.
19	Irreplaceable	Exceptional, unique regards
20	Consistency	To wrestle, surrender, and receive a better, different, and fulfilling outcome.

ABOUT THE AUTHOR

Leona Phillips Jackson looks forward to uncovering and discovering more knowledge concerning Spiritual Wellness and Spiritual Illness. So many of her quality skills, including the craft of writing, were an ultimate surprise to Ms. Jackson. Yet, when all else failed again, she found another source of light, learning, and living through writing.

In the years ahead, Ms. Jackson will be researching talks about getting to know self-better: Self-Discipline, Self-Care, Self-Respect, Self-Survival, Self-Assurance, Self-Belief, Self-Trust, Self-Love, Self-Breakthroughs, Self-Amends, Self-Understanding, Self-Forgiveness, Self-Image, Self-Praise, Self-Development, Self-Support, Self-Progress, Self-Growth, Self-Confidence, Self-Guidance, Self-Worth, Self-Wealth and overall Self-Improvement, to embrace and to pass on to yet other self-starved, self-depleted and self-ignored persons.

Ms. Jackson retired as an Office Assistant III from the University of Washington. She re-entered the work world in 2011 with Allied Universal Security. She enjoys writing and attends classes daily to become an Empathic and Financial Coach.

Ms. Jackson is a mom of two adult children, Richard and Secret. In addition, even at 78, she still works forty-plus hours a week. Ms. Jackson spends her leisure time supporting small groups, striving to learn more about assembling Diverse teams and Self-management skills, and at the same time, Ms. Jackson is racing for a seat at the Diversity, Equity, Ethics, and Inclusion tables. She still thrives to become worthy of her calling while examining her brand, purpose, and niche! She is the author of four books. *Release Me*, *The Spirit of Becoming*, *A Story to Tell*, and her most recent book, *The Coach Within*, to be released soon!

www.ingramcontent.com/pod-product-compliance
Lightning Source LLC
Chambersburg PA
CBHW051219120626
46547CB00013B/1420